AUTUMN DAYS

BRIDGING CHANGE

KATHERINE EDWINS SCHUMM

ISBN: 1480010766

ISBN-13: 978-1480010765

DEDICATION

My father taught me the importance of stories. He told them
incessantly, as if he were giving me the most important lessons
of life. My mother learned how to accept change with dignity
and how to make life meaningful in the presence of an ever
changing and shrinking world. It has inspired me. My husband,
who pays attention to every finite detail, stepped in to help me
when I needed direction. My children taught me how to
stay fresh and to see things with new eyes. They challenged
the status quo I was holding onto so tightly.

How lucky I am to have all these teachers.

I hope my stories mentor you as you
create a new life in your autumn days.

ACKNOWLEDGEMENTS

Author's Photo: Photography by M J Schaub

My dear friend and amazing photographer

Cover Photo – Katherine Edwins Schumm

Autumn bridge in Burnsville, Minnesota

Editing: Gayle Smith

Cover Matters: Claudette Parmenter

These two wonderful women were my sounding boards

as I began the assembly of this work.

Thanks as well to my writing group who

encouraged me to see these essays as a whole work.

"I cannot change the world,

but I can cast a stone across the waters

to create many ripples."

Mother Teresa

Autumn Days – Table of Contents

Introduction

"When I retire I will never set my alarm clock...I will never wear a suit again...I will...NOT...." The theme repeated itself often as I interviewed retirees. The negative perspective surprised me. According to the Bureau of the Census most of us will live 20-30 years in retirement before we need assistance.

I was inspired to write this book as I watched my 90-year-old mother transition from an active, independent, busy life to one which is dependent on others. It has been an incredible mountain to climb. She didn't see it coming. What does she need in this new life to make it zesty and meaningful rather than just a waiting room for death? I began to ask other seniors about their plans. How do they see their transition from work to retirement? What are the problems they encounter and how do they solve them? What do they wish they had known before it happened? The issues that surfaced are about creating new friendships, finding meaningful things to do, dealing with illnesses and assessing their spiritual beliefs and more.

What we do with other life transitions is to set long term and short term goals. We make a plan for what we are going to do and we put it in writing. We don't do that for retirement except for the "financial plan". We wing the rest. It is as if retirement is not the same as a career, or child planning. We do not plan our careers or anything else from a negative slant, certainly. Now is the time to plan from a positive outlook.

This book is not a "how to" book in the sense that you are given instructions. It is a montage of thoughts, reflections and stories that might start you thinking about how to create a great new life without having to sail on a Sargasso Sea. My hope is that you can laugh and cry, think and dream as you step into the process. This is the time we have all waited for, "just going fishing," will not be enough. Begin. The rest is easy.

"Some changes look negative on the surface, but you will soon realize that space is being created in your life for something new to emerge. " Eckhart Tolle

August Days

August was my grandfather's name. In his early thirty's, a small town preacher in Stillwater, Minnesota, he married a girl fifteen years his junior and left the country to answer God's call in China. He was an introvert by all accounts. A scholar, his library was full of books and he was accomplished in Latin and Greek. He decided to translate the Bible into Mandarin. He played the violin, wrote short articles for the American mission churches and prayed. Yes, he preached and converted as well. My more pragmatic grandmother managed the household, which eventually included 11 children, various servants and other missionary families who came to the red clay hills of Henan. I mention all of this because, though I didn't ever get to meet him, I felt inspired by the part of him who was the adventurer.

August in Minnesota, as well as the green forested mountains of Henan, is the time when nature begins to don a coat of riotous color. An abandoned celebration in the ripe fields and pumpkin forests, reminds us to celebrate the full potential which has grown from the spring and summer plantings. Autumn, however luscious, also carries in its maw a shadow of what will follow in the gray and brown of winter. It is a last full season to jump for joy in crisp piles of dusty leaves; to cover fall apples with rich brown caramel and yourself in comforting heavy flannels.

The metaphor for me is that this zesty, fulfilling time parallel's my own life's journey. These are the August days of my life and I am reminded to show up and be present in the moment, as it is a finite time. The first cold, wet storm of illness or the creaking slowness of knees and hips is the specter we meet in the crossroads of autumn. This is the moment to do what we have left undone and gather the ripe fruits of our lives, to share them with those who have not yet left the spring or summer of theirs. My grandfather's August was cut short. As a prisoner of the Japanese and with a heart which was not strong enough to endure, his autumn ended too soon. The lesson for me is to find a joyful heart and celebrate.

The seeds of this book have come in the days, which mark my retirement: my mother's slowing abilities and my sense that lurking somewhere in the shadows is winter. I see life so differently from when I was younger. I am now happy in my dream pursuits, all the things I wanted to do on my bucket list. I love that I have many new friends who talk about what is meaningful to them and to me. I think about death and life. I think about what death will look like and what my spiritual self needs. I revel in the insights that are coming to my grandchildren as they learn about becoming individuals away from their parents. My husband and I can be busy at different things and enjoy talking about them at the end of our day. We can laugh at the neighbor mowing his lawn shirtless in his black socks and wingtips. I can drive twenty miles an hour on the roads without feeling like jumping out of my skin. This is an uncharted territory for me and I am exploring each day with new eyes. My stories are about this new autumn and my thoughts as I experience the changes.

Autumn is always my favorite time of the year.

"The world as we have created it is a process of our thinking. It cannot be changed without changing our thinking"

Albert Einstein

Change

The very process of birth is an act of change. We cannot choose the time of our birth or the circumstances. Look at the changes you have made in your life, some were voluntary and some were forced on you by random circumstance. What differentiates change from powerlessness?

Retiring can be something that happens to you by downsizing or it can be a decision you make in your own thoughtful process. It requires a creative act of taking power and making the opportunity work for you. Remember you have many choices and you can choose to make them. You are not powerless; you are powerful beyond what you believe.

Take the time to write down what the changes are you want and what you want them to look like. Use the energy it creates to be your own agent of transformation. Grandma Moses began to paint at the age of 76 long after many of us leave work. She became a self-made, powerful woman at a time when many of us would choose to sit on the porch and drink tea.

Questions

*How does **change** feel right now?*

How am I dealing with it?

*Am I using **change** to redefine myself or does it define me?*

Action

Write down your goals for change.

Two Cups on The Windowsill

Each morning was the same. They were both morning people, so Cleo made the bed while David got the newspaper. The house filled with the heavy smell of freshly brewed coffee. She would enter the small kitchen, take down the Tuesday cups, or whatever day it was, and fill them. Sitting down, she would wait for him at the small table. The maple table was one of the few remaining furniture pieces from their early marriage but it was perfect in their tiny kitchen.

Breakfast was a piece of wheat toast each, covered with white and yellow cheese accompanied by the fruit of the day. The first order was to eat their breakfast and play a hand of gin rummy. Early in their marriage they kept score. No matter where they were, the scorecard and the cards were part of their day together. Now, after sixty-five years, they no longer kept score but played and munched, laughed and planned their day. Breakfast dishes put away, David opened his father's Bible and they had their daily devotions. It was a way for them to anchor the day as well as nurture their relationship before they were caught in the swift current of their activities.

I am not sure in the busy wash of life many of us have such a strong set of rituals. Family, work, activities fill our calendars with the speed of a tsunami. Rituals may be in a long commute, reading the paper or a short game of golf. Time becomes our most valuable commodity. Friendships and relationships like Dave and Cleo's were anchored in the nurture of whatever little rituals they could manage.

In the end, David died and Cleo was tucked safely into a new life where she is content. The silent kitchen still had stories to tell. One cupboard alone spoke the loudest. An odd collection of mugs occupied one shelf and to the casual observer it was a hodge-podge of colors and patterns in twos, as if they couldn't afford to buy a matching set. The two blue Navy mugs were for Monday, given to them by their youngest son while he was in Vietnam and who preceded them in death. Red pottery mugs, solid and substantial, with white hearts from a family visit to Norway on the Sognefjord were the Wednesday cups. Each pair marked a memory or person in this morning ritual.

The sun creeps across the empty room and settles on the opposite side of the room. On the windowsill sit two blue and white cups with graceful fluid Koi swimming toward nowhere in particular, these were Sunday's cups. Now, each day Cleo still gets up early and makes her bed. Her little room in the senior living facility forces her to live "smaller". Green tea has become her morning beverage, warmed in the microwave next to the treasured maple table. Each day she follows a similar routine as before, this time without David. Monday, the Navy mug and when it is time, she and her walker head down to the dining room for breakfast with strangers.

*"You are never too old to set another goal
or to dream a new dream."*

C.S. Lewis

Ritual

Ritual is a way to order our days, to find a structure for our lives. It helps create a framework when you retire or experience big changes. We are comforted by daily routines. We brush our teeth, take a shower, and we have something to eat or a cappuccino. Ritual is a meaningful repetition.

During change each of us is faced with a large unstructured block of time. This is the blank canvass we have been waiting for all our lives. Just as you planned your day with work, the best use of this wonderful opportunity is to create things to "anchor" your days.

Ritual is also a way to keep us moving. Since we are not accustomed to the lack of structure, we need a way to wrangle it into shape. Many people find themselves confounded and become frozen; they sleep all day or watch TV, get bored or depressed.

What kind of ritual can you establish to frame each day? One of my neighbors gets up each morning and showers immediately, does her hair and puts on her makeup. Personally, I like slower mornings with a cup of coffee and the paper while in my pajamas and I may not shower until I have to do something that involves other people.

Questions

What will help you find your rhythm?

How can you create your own order?

Actions

Create a ritual or write down your daily rituals.

Making Change at the Grocery Store

It is not fair to give the grocery store all the credit. It just happens to be where I was when this newest epiphany came to me. If I remember correctly, I have always been annoyed by the "little old lady" who spent time at a busy check out counter counting out the change from her teeny tiny coin purse! I have a busy life after all, just get me the heck out of Dodge! Looking for that third penny in a pile of nickels and dimes just sets me into a stew of frustration and itchiness. *Come'on already, give her a nickel and get change! Let me give you a nickel and keep the change. I'm late for work or I need to get supper on the table when I get home – whatever. What is it with old people anyway? Beside which, they obviously don't have jobs, why don't they shop in the middle of the week? In the middle of the day?*

I do not go to the grocery store very often. Usually my husband wants to go and I never argue. There are, however, times when I am forced to enter those doors and get into the fray whether I want to or not.

I wasn't alone. A friend and I had just been to lunch and decided to stop to pick up just a few items. It was Saturday of course. Well, because. Well, I am not sure why. We are both retired, very busy women, given where we live. We are trying to make up for all the days in our life when we wished we could play bridge in the middle of the day, tee off at 10 a.m. or go to yoga and follow it up with an afternoon nap. We earned the right to do what we want, when we want. It says so in the lifestyle magazine published each month in our area. We are entitled. This is our time to play.

I quickly found the dairy section and grabbed the small box of cheese I needed. My friend grabbed a magazine while she waited. It was an impulse purchase I could see. The check out lady was someone I occasionally see at the pool. She is such a darling! She smiled and asked me - "Did I find everything I was looking for? Was this all I needed? Have I been to the pool recently? How do I like this rainy weather?" The joy of living in a small town. Everyone is so friendly. After those few amenities she told me my total was $2.64.

I sure wasn't going to charge it to my credit card, after all, it was such a small amount. I dug in my purse, moving aside my keys, the notes I had put there before leaving home to remind me about checking the mail on the way home, the new tube of lip gloss that I had bought yesterday at the dollar store. I finally came upon my wallet and began looking for money. I realized that this new "lifestyle" included not carrying around much cash in my pocketbook. My husband carries the money and pays so that I don't have to bother with such trivia.

I found only a one dollar bill, but lots of change. I was sure I could come up with enough, so I started digging. I came up with three quarters and five dimes…let's see…what does that make? Hummm…$1.25 plus the $1.00 so I am close. I only need, let's see sixty-four minus twenty-five is, so I started counting on my fingers. What more did I need?

My friendly check out person was getting just a little "twitchy". My friend was nervously looking behind her at the six people who had just come to stand in our lane. Crimminy…there were other lanes. Did I have enough? I wasn't a math major after all. I figured I needed another thirty-nine cents and there was still lots of change in my teeny tiny little coin purse. I dumped the coins out onto the counter to see if I could come up with the missing change.

At that moment, my friend couldn't contain herself one more minute. "For goodness sake, Katherine! Here are two quarters, let's get this over and get out of here! The woman behind me in the line, with half the grocery store in her cart is about to blow up. Her face is turning red, her eyes have begun to bulge."

What? Why are people so impatient? I just wanted to use up the change in my purse and it didn't seem like it took that long! Manners! People just don't have them any more.

"OK, OK, I'm moving!"

Journal of Changes

I was taught never to write in my books, or to turn down the corners. Books were sacrosanct and I still have many of them on my bookshelf as crisp and new as they were when I bought them fifty years ago.

I realized, finally, they were mine and they were my friends. I loved them like the velveteen rabbit and if they were to become a real part of my life I needed to claim them. I began by underlining in pencil. I was very tidy, mind you, and I still never turn down the corners.

I needed more however, so writing notes on the margins when I had an "aha" moment seemed important to my finding all the spicy, zesty thoughts later. Now these friends sit waiting for me on my bookcase and when I need them, I can find the best parts quickly.

Action

Here is a blank space. Write what you want.

Broken Versus Transformed

Is broken bad? Is it forever? Is there ever redemption from broken? Do we see others or ourselves as broken?

The questions arise out of a story of two pots used by a poor man to carry water from the creek to his home. One pot, slightly cracked, leaks and on arrival home the man has less water than if both his pots were whole.

If it were your pot, would you get a new one? Would you throw away the broken one? Our answers may be different.

I never throw anything away. The metaphor for me is transformation. I would find a way to make it new again, to fix it, to reuse it in a different way, to re-vision the pot. All of this makes sense when you know that I am a mosaic artist. I break perfectly good things and then put them back together to make other perfectly good things. I see the broken pot as an opportunity.

Recently someone told me a story about the shame she carried all her life. A shame born from her mother's refrain, "You will never amount to anything". She felt broken without exactly knowing why.

Eighty years under her belt, a lifetime of accomplishments and she still heard her mother's voice "you are broken". She raised three exemplary children; had been happily married for sixty years; had entertained heads of state with ease and grace and had traveled the world. Yet, in the mirror of her life, she still sees the cracks and imperfections of her mother's regard.

Everyday I take old beautiful plates and cups and smash them to bits. These shards become new again in my mosaic creations. Grandma's old chipped and cracked plate transforms into a new and precious tabletop in my mother's apartment. Each day she and a friend share a glass of wine and crackers with the table between them. Everyone who sees the table is charmed by the history and its loveliness. Never does someone see the brokenness – they only see the beauty.

The story continues as the pot, ashamed of its brokenness, apologizes to the old man. The man's answer is a surprise. He tells the pot that the leaking water nourishes and encourages flowers to grow along his path. As he does this daily ritual of carrying water for his family, the flowers transform a daily chore to a joyful vista.

Is broken bad?

We are all broken in one way or another and that brokenness allows transformation. Each of us can build from the shards, a life which is stronger, unique and more valuable than before. It is because of the cracks and chips that we are beautiful. As with the pot, we water the creative seeds of "self" and decorate the side of the road on which all of us travel.

Every blade of grass has its angel that bends over it and whispers, "grow, grow."

The Talmud

Wholeness

At this stage we each carry the traumas and pains we experienced in our lives. We raised children, built careers and took care of the details of life. We tucked those little pains away for a time when they can be addressed. Suddenly, as the responsibilities go away, the old cracks become more pressing.

It used to be the practice to bury old automobile tires in the "dump". They would be carefully covered with dirt to tidy up the area in the hopes that they would go away and keep our landscapes beautiful. Unfortunately, you can't bury a tire successfully. When it rains and the water percolates into the earth, the hydraulics of physics, pushes them upward inexorably to the surface. You can't bury a tire, you need to transform it.

The cracks and chips that you have stored in the attic of your life are part of the necessary change. Eventually they scream for your attention. They need to be transformed. They need to be recycled into something positive so you can be whole and new again yourself.

Questions

What is getting in the way of your happiness or wholeness?

What are you going to make of those things?

Action

Make a repair list and address them.

Silence at Three

Nothing is as dark and silent as the garden at three in the morning. The dogs head out at that hour with the same 'joie de vivre' as they do in the middle of the day. It would seem to anyone who isn't owned by a dog that it is an impertinence to be out sniffing and peeing in the dark of that hour.

Of course, there are various kinds of dark, depending how close or far you live from the city. When the only light is the moon, and the stars are so bright and crisp that you can reach out and touch Cassiopeia, you can call yourself lucky. The soul who is allowed to stand barefoot in the lush carpet of dark grass wearing little but jammies is nourished in the darkness. It is hard to fathom how just stepping into the darkness can scare so many. On reflection it is understandable, given how foreign that experience has become. This occasional forced dark meditation is a blessing and I am awed with how amazing the stars look in the dark night sky.

Our lives are lived at breakneck speed amid a cacophony of sound and light. The norm, for the most part, is to sit behind drawn shades with the TV or music filling our ears and pot lights scaring away the demons. The black velvet pall of night hides all the things that go bump in the night. What is it that scares us?

Is it a metaphorical darkness that frightens us? Could it be the darkness of our minds and the shadow of death, no matter our age? It makes us inclined to close the blinds, turn up the volume and hope that it will not tap us on the shoulder. I feel a sobering grief that the coming generations might live only with noise and light. They will never recognize both the silence and the darkness as an endangered, precious gift. If we ever expect answers to all the questions we face everyday, how will we hear them if we never introduce ourselves to the silence that allows "inner-speak" or "God Answers"?

At the insistent whimpering of "Big Red", I grab a wrap and tiptoe out of the bedroom. Ever so carefully I turn the latch on the door and step out into the garden. The great horned owl nearby complains about my disturbing presence while the dog checks the yard and does her business. I settle into a lawn chair as the world sleeps. I wrap the blanket tighter around my shoulders and begin counting the stars.

> *Listening looks easy, but it's not simple.*
> *Every head is a world."*   *Cuban Proverb*

Listening

Anyone who wears hearing aids understands why they are a mixed blessing. We have put men on the moon but we still do not have the technology to drown out extraneous sound. Ask someone who is hard of hearing. In the sports bars where four or five TV's blast three different kinds of sporting events we are bombarded with sound. It means we are not required to talk to one another. The other side of the story is if someone is terminally boring at the table you can surreptitiously turn the aids off. All of us know what I'm saying.

There is very little silence anymore. I think back to my grandparents farm yard. Walking in the dark back to the house from the barn was silent. The kind of silence which is deafening. Darkness so deep that you welcome the dim light from the kitchen window which guides your path. It is the kind of experience which no longer exists in the urban and suburban setting.

Noise is a powerful way to numb the brain. Noise excuses us from dealing with the sounds inside our heads. We think if we turn up the radio we will no longer be lonely, sad, empty or whatever!

Questions

What comes to you out of the silence?

How do you experience darkness?

Action

Be quiet for a few moments each day.

How to Become A Hoarder in 5 Easy Steps

Really, it took me years to discover that I was a hoarder. I might say I am a pretty good one. In fact, I didn't know there was a name for it until I saw the TV show. They haven't called me from the program yet, but I have sent them both my cell and home numbers. I am certain they will want me.

I was thinking about this incredible and unappreciated talent that I exhibit. It suddenly came to me, a 'bolt out of the blue', so to speak. Pure genius! *Other people might want to have some 'how to' information so they can be like me or at least have the tools to emulate me.* In the spirit of sharing here are my steps.

My Five Easy Steps.

Step One: You must have parents or family who grew up during the Great Depression. You get extra credit toward success if said parents have some interesting, quirky socioeconomic differences from all the "normal" parents out there. I was lucky enough to have come from good Norwegian stock with a short stopover on my father's side in Sweden. "Waste not, want not" was their mantra. I learned early that absolutely everything had value – my grandmother saved everything including the squeak from the pig! Thus, step one is inherited – ya gotta be lucky here. If not, you could move out on the family tree until you find someone who went thru the Great Depression. Don't give up – most families have skeletons lurking somewhere.

Step Two: You have to be an enthusiastic and dedicated learner. The messages from our GD families - hang on, that GD stands for Great Depression - have to make an impression. Not everyone can be converted to the singular understanding that even the simplest things can be the beginning of our own stash. My father, owner of a small business, believed that in some decade or desperate situation he might need the date stamp from the envelope of a water bill or telephone bill. When he died, my poor brother had to take 30 years of envelopes and the invoices to the shredder. Dad never needed them, but if he had, he would have been able to prove that the August bill in 1963 was mailed on the 15th of the month and not the 5th. I listened carefully. I believed. After 20 years living alone, I moved and had to take many boxes to the shredder. My goofy brother throws everything. Cheez – he had the same opportunity as I did, but he threw it away.

Step Three: Be a collector. It feels more "upscale" and takes you out of the realm of being quirky or crazy. I am not just talking envelopes here. I am talking about serious stuff. Personally I like plates, saucers, and cups, with odd and interesting patterns. I am also fond of refrigerator art from children, mine obviously and odd photos of forgotten families and neighbors at Christmas. You get the idea. What? You never heard of Emelda Marcos? She collected! Her thing was shoes for goodness sake, and how many of those can you wear at one time? She was never given the title of hoarder. If you are rich, you are given more leeway. A friend in my neighborhood collects snow globes. She has hundreds. It is not like she will ever need them, she just likes them and wants them. Can't get enough of them. Hoarding is not totally random, folks. You have to love the stuff you keep.

Step Four: I will spell this one out for you. Pay Attention. C.A.M.O.F.L.A.G.E!!! I dare any woman reading this to tell me she never brought some new outfits home from the store, cut off the tags, hung them randomly throughout the closet and destroyed the evidence!!! I'm talking the receipt, the bag, and the tissue. Girls, I know the secret – you just tell your husband/partner that it is something you have had for a while. 'For a while' is the operative word and can mean anything from

10 minutes to two years. That is our little secret. When you run out of storage in the closet, remember the guest closet, under the bed, the linen closet or anywhere no one will notice that you are stockpiling.

A neighbor suggested to me the other day that I turn my guest room into a "study/craft/writing" room by removing the bed and replacing it with a sleeper couch. Really, people! There are amazing storage possibilities under every bed. Obviously my neighbor came out of the same, clean, tidy school that my brother did!

I have stashes of those little yellow sticky pads left when my husband sold his business. I hope to use some of them as a famous author to bookmark the brilliant things I have written. Right now they are crammed into one of those pretty photo boxes on the closet shelf next to my old college texts from freshman year. I might need them if I ever go back to teaching. A designer box makes the shelf look stylishly "shabby chic" and hides its true function.

Step Five: I guess that is only four steps. I was going to suggest that step #5 was to find a twelve-step program, but some friends and I are going thrifting. Hope that I find some old dishes while I'm at it. Maybe my helpful neighbor will store them for me.

* * *

I trust this information has been useful to you. I wish you success in your endeavors. Some of us have got it and some of us have to work at it. Keep on trying.

Regards, xoxo

Stuff

You know what I am talking about. Stuff can be a tyrant, hiding in the corners of our homes. I will admit there are people who can easily throw everything and start fresh without batting an eyelash. I think their numbers are pretty small compared to those of us who have saved Grandma's dishes and wine goblets. We, who love the old black and multicolored afghan our old maiden aunt made us which sits on the hope chest that grandma brought with her from Norway, can't give away.

Retirement is a new life. In downsizing we realize our children don't want the things we have saved. Whatever your retirement looks like, this is the time. It is the time to give it away or sell it. Our children value stainless steel over sterling silver especially as it does not need polishing. What are you holding on to that is not valued by anyone but yourself?

You cannot find new things for your life when your hands are full of the old stuff. Let go, and skinny dip in your life. See how liberating it can be.

Questions

Am I a prisoner of my things?

What do I want and what do I need?

Action

Give away one thing a day.

How Deep?

The images of strong, athletic divers jumping from the jagged cliffs of Mexico into the dark and angry water of the sea below, put me in a cold sweat. I hate heights in the first place and could never step out onto the rock ledge at such a dizzying spot. To step off that ledge and plunge into a small patch of frothy ocean is more courage than I believe I have.

At some time in each of our lives we have to metaphorically step off into the unknown. Until that very moment, we have no idea how deep we can reach. Each of us would rather stay on the safe path, take fewer risks and play life from a comfortable perch. Safety is never guaranteed in our lives. Some random, universal cataclysm can pitch us off balance and force us to jump. At that point we discover how resourceful we can be.

The morning of September 11th, 2001 was such a morning. Ordinary people woke to the dawn and were drawn into the horrible circumstances of the day. They were compelled to find their depth. The amazing stories of valor on that single day inspire us even now years later.

Recently a commercial airline pilot, faced with the choice of a catastrophe or some amazingly pragmatic thinking, landed in the Hudson River. The situation tested his faith, his skill, his experience and his ability to think quickly and creatively. The decision he made was pure genius and saved hundreds of lives. These are the extraordinary events which awe and inspire us when we hear the stories.

In reality these are ordinary people doing extraordinary things. We, as they have, each come to our own individual challenges. Not someone else but me. Am I ready? What will I do?

I heard a story about a man and woman who were rendered helpless by a quirk of circumstance. A terrible accident ended her life and her husband was in a coma for an extended time. They were not able to make choices; the choices were made for them. It fell to their young daughter, who by her own words, wanted to run and hide in the face of such cruel responsibility. At that very moment, the person she thought she was, changed. She stepped up and found her depth however uncertain she felt and she persevered.

History is what happens while we are living our days. Every moment schools us for competence, for bravery and courage. None of us wishes to be tested like these people. We can hope our work and the experiences will carry us. You never know.

We will not know the answer until we face the darkness and shine our light.

Elizabeth Kubler Ross said – "People are like stained glass windows. They are beautiful in the sunlight, but when the darkness comes, their true beauty is revealed only if there is a light from within."

When you face the darkness, may you shine.

Strength

Each day, we don't know what kind of crisis we will have to meet. Inevitably each of us will be called upon to be strong. None of us gets out of this opportunity. We all have to trust our skills and apply them in that moment.

I think back to the shooting death of John Fitzgerald Kennedy. The whole nation grieved. Mrs. Kennedy showed us how to be courageous. We collectively believed that if she could do this, so could we. She was a victim but became a teacher.

We thought it was the most horrific thing that could ever happen to us as a nation. We were wrong. The 9/11 terror was beyond belief, but that day we became a community. We helped each other and gathered our strength for a common goal – to protect America. We have it in us.

Questions

What will help you be strong in a crisis?

What skills will you call on?

Action

Write a list of your personal emergency strengths.

I See Dead People

The last thing you should ever say to someone on the slippery slope of sixty-five is anything about death! In retirement communities is it tantamount to saying the "F" word or discussing "STD's". If death happens, it only occurs in the most subtle and euphemistic ways imaginable.

In polite circles it is expected one would don their most solemn face and say, preceded by a breathless pause, "she passed". Or, "my neighbor 'lost' her husband the other day". The reciprocal protocol then requires a knowing roll of the eyes to the heavens followed by a remark similar to "poor dear".

When we were in our thirties we sent sympathy cards. In our 50's it was the cause for a tuna noodle hot dish or pan of brownies. Now, in our "later years"…well, let's be truthful, no one ever passes until it becomes a blessing of some kind. "She had been ill for so long, it was a blessing." Alternatively one might say, "He died on the 8th green after just shooting a hole-in-one, it was a blessing."

The paradox of all of this is the cemetery in our senior community. No one really knows because it has been effectively camouflaged. Thick hedges of bamboo and sweet viburnum grow around it, decorated by beds of brightly colored plants. Truthfully, if you are clever enough you don't even have to glance in that direction, kind of a senior citizen ostrich reaction.

Cemeteries have always fascinated me. When I was younger I loved wandering through them reading the headstones. Near my grandparents home, the rural church was within walking distance and we would play "hide-and-seek" there to escape the chores our mothers always thought we should be doing. Now at sixty, I am still curious enough to take a look at the "hidden" cemetery.

This cemetery is an old one and used to be part of an AME church in the area. In the 60's, the church was burned down. The cemetery, however, stands as a monument to the congregation and to those they loved. Undeterred by the bamboo, one afternoon I climbed the fence and dodged the undergrowth. It was a lovely, quiet place with old trees and even older headstones. History leached out of every stone and hung in silent testament from the moss covered live oaks. Well before our parents and our grandparents were born, there were families burying their loved ones here. I imagined I could hear the voices of remembrance wafting on the light breeze that wandered down the dirt trail to the east.

I know that those who rest here will not hurt me. The stones tell stories of families, their loves, losses, struggles and sadness. It reminds us that we are all marching irrevocably toward a meeting with all who came before.

At my age, I have accomplished much and have little to regret. I still have things to do, but I want to have death find me like Mary Oliver's poem: "When Death Comes":

"When death comes.........I want to step through the door of curiosity...into that cottage of darkness. When it is over, I want to say "all my life I was a bride married to amazement....I don't want to end up simply having visited this world."

Endings

I have never understood how some people can thumb to the end of a book and read it out of order. Why would you want to know the end before you know the beginning and the middle? Many people do it, however. Fortunetellers and psychics make a lot of money foreshadowing the end to anxious customers. Some authors will even satisfy this voyeuristic tendency by starting with the end and then skipping back to the beginning.

Our lives are only truly a book when the end is finally written. We can never skip ahead. The story is for someone else to tell.

We can control the end only in small details. We can tell those close to us what we want and hope they honor it. Mary Oliver was not talking about the end exactly. She was talking about the journey. The end is only remarkable if the journey was meaningful. This is it, friend. You are currently writing the chapter, which may be continued or may be the last.

Questions

What would you hope your epitaph will say about you?

What can you do now to make it remarkable?

Action

Make a bucket list.

The Great Gyre

Hong Kong harbor in 1998 had changed so much from when I lived there in the 50's. The few familiar things left were the Star Ferries plying back and forth from Hong Kong Island to the New Territories and the clock tower on the Kowloon side. Forty years of growth had changed it from a lovely harbor town to a megatropolis crowded with people. Our hotel room looked out over the harbor. Sitting by the window in the early light of morning with my cappuccino, I could see little knots of men in bathing suits and white towels, probably businessmen, walking along the quay. Dropping their towels on the cement wall, they climbed down into the water of the harbor for their morning swim. It made me gag to think of getting into the flotsam and jetsam of that salty cesspool. This culture never did honor the ocean but thought of it as a huge garbage disposal. Surely any of us who live in a highly pasteurized world would spend a few days in the hospital after a swim like that? The new millennium and cultural changes have awakened Asia to the environment. Recycling has become economically necessary and financially advantageous, so things are changing.

Now, I wake up in a central Florida village. It is a world away from my work. Life is different in retirement and I am involved in new things. I explored joining the "Baby Boomers" club, but I guess I am too old; you have to have been born after 1946. I'm out. It's all right though, I am close and I believe my lifestyle and values are the same as theirs. We were the generation who cared about social issues. We marched for every cause imaginable – civil rights, the war, and peace. You named a cause and people showed up in their political tee shirts and we marched. Our community is 95,000 people strong, mostly college educated, and we religiously keep up with current events. We adopt causes from the nearby communities for the disadvantaged; we share food for Thanksgiving and gather gifts for poverty level children at Christmas. We look out for our neighbors and bring chicken soup when they are ill. We sit with them when someone they love is ill. A young author from the north wrote that seniors in planned communities check out of life. He was wrong. We still care and are actively involved in things around us. I am so proud to give back to the next generation as I enjoy a new life away from ice and snow.

In places on the globe we can't see or even imagine, there are things called "Gyres". They are islands of garbage, largely a mix of pelagic plastic and chemical sludge, larger than twice the size of the United States. They float in the ocean caught by currents and attest to the fact that we are slow to change old habits. It makes sense to me that "they", the third world countries who don't know any better have been the cause of this mess. I like this moral high ground, as my community is pristine. None of us pollute or litter.

P.S. Did you know that fewer than half of the senior residents in my community recycle? What's with that? For more information check this out:

[http://en.wikipedia.org/wiki/Great_Pacific_Garbage_Patch]

"Listen up, you couch potatoes: each recycled can saves enough electricity to run a television for three hours."

Denis Hayes

Recycling

What's your plan?

Behind The Pine Tree Curtain

People who live in different areas of the country are odd to be sure. The mores are certainly off the scale in the Midwest so I have taken it upon myself to share with you, life on the prairie. We can all learn something from this kind of diversity training. If you should ever find yourself in need of adjusting to life in the prairie states, here are some tips.

What To Wear: On any given day in the land of the tall prairie grass you can show up in your best plaid flannel shirt, your new hunting boots and fit right in. I have cousins who have two pair of hunting boots, one for work and one for dress. After all, their kin came across the long prairies of Ohio and Wisconsin under great duress what with freezing temperatures and hostile natives. They moved into houses built into the side of a pasture with sod walls and roofs. You thought that "Little House on the Prairie" was fiction? Guess again. When my third cousin got married she wore her best cowgirl boots under her mother's wedding dress. The best man wore the suit that they bought earlier that year to bury his daddy in. Of course his daddy was still with us, but they knew that one wearing of the suit wouldn't bother daddy when he passed. Sure there are city slickers in the Midwest, but they don't count much. The salt of the earth live in the country after all.

Church – The Community Center : There is no dancing and drinking anytime in the church basement. There is some misbehaving, usually reserved for the men who go out to the cemetery away from the women and children. You gotta put up the right attitude when in a sanctified space such as a church or a funeral home! The ladies aid will serve a mighty fine meal. If you are lucky, one of the local women will bring her best dish of Tuna Noodle Casserole, now there is a dish popular with the flannel set! Mostly, if you live in a German or Scandinavian neighborhood, the food will be white and the beverage will be cherry. The cherry nectar will give you some color on the table next to the pastor's wife's flowers picked out of her garden and stuck in a vase from the funeral last week. We have certain standards to maintain. I understand that in some of the middle European communities they allow beer in the basement when they have bingo games but it is only hinted at in some of the ladies circles

Education: They are pretty much doing away with the one-room schoolhouse these days due to budget cuts. It is a mighty shame if you ask me. My mother walked to school most days, up hill in both directions with only bread bags on her shoes. At least that is what she tells me all the time. The school -teacher lived with local families for three months at a time. When she stayed with my grandparents, my grandpa would allow her to hitch up one of the draft horses to the buggy and the kids would get to ride to school. The teacher was usually a person regarded with some awe sprinkled in with some pity. After all, she had no man, which was considered a grievous character flaw. She was dependent on the folks around for her room and board. Most were grateful that their children got an education but they made sure the teacher knew that if the crops needed tending, there would be fewer children in the classroom that day. These days the children are bussed many miles to the local school. They arrive home late for the milking and other chores. What an inconvenience for the parents. The new big shot principal from the city declared that students missing more than four days of school in one semester would get an automatic failing grade. Poor Dr. Dodson has been hard pressed to write hundreds of excuse letters for ailing kids who were actually working out in the fields.

Women-folk: Normally a well-heeled country person would not discuss such sensitive things, but here's another head turner. I beg your forgiveness for my audacity. Most women have never had a manicure, much less a pedicure. Wax was used in the kitchen for sealing up preserves and making candles. It certainly was not for the unimaginable things that have been hinted in one of the magazines at the Thompton's grocery store while you wait in line to check out your purchases! Blows my mind to think of what those city women do with their left-over wax when they don't need it for canning etc. It is just unnatural if you ask me.

Men-stuff: Like I said, men are different out here. Living off the land can be a solitary thing and they must be able to fix anything. What is so striking about country men is they count on one another. They have "man-klatches". You know what I mean? Like the smoke breaks and joke telling out in the cemetery while the women are making their white food. Never, I say never however, mess with his hat! It is his own quirky fashion statement. You can always tell a country man by his white forehead and bad hair. Used to be a time when a man would take his hat off in the house or the store, but not now. The hat is stylin' – like if it says John Deere" you know him; if it has an American Flag you understand him. Yup, and if it says "Ping", well, he is a tourist for sure.

* * *

Well, gotta go now. Millie Torvold's coming over to help me put up all those chickens that Charlie stashed out in the barn. Nothing like a good chicken stew for dinner in the middle of a harsh Minnesota winter. I gotta find my best flannel apron so I don't get blood on my nice new house dress. Millie said afterward we could watch a movie her daughter brought home from college. Guess it is one of those reality shows called *Fargo* and they tell a wicked story about how we live out here. For heavens sake, what are they teaching children in college these days? Uff da.

Laughter

Shortly after we were married, my family gave my husband a subscription to "Readers Digest" for his birthday. How he loved getting his copy each month. How I dreaded it . Why, you ask? He never looked at the articles. He read each and every joke four or five times to anyone within ear shot. Whatever I was doing, he would follow me around the house reading jokes. "Just one more,or you just have to hear this one!" He did that for the neighbor mowing his lawn or the mailman . He laughed every time, even if it was for the fifth time. When the kids were old enough, he would sit at the dinner table and read them to the kids. When the kids were old enough to get the "Weekly Reader" they would read him the jokes at dinner. I remember a lot of laughter.

My husband went to the doctor's office recently in a great deal of pain. Bored and anxious he grabbed a magazine. Shazam! It was not the "Readers Digest", but it was full of silly jokes. He began to chuckle and said, "ya gotta hear this one". Pretty soon we were sitting side by side in a tiny cubicle laughing our heads off. When had we stopped reading jokes to one another? When was the last time we laughed – I mean really laughed? The nurse came in to see if we were OK, we both smiled. We felt better. We felt more in unison and happy. I wonder if I can still get a subscription for laughter somewhere on this planet?

Questions

Are you taking vitamins in place of laughing?

Action

Laugh, laugh, laugh!

Forgiveness

I have made some uncomfortable discoveries about myself. I live by a fairly strict set of rules. Rules I made up. The surprise for me is those rules are malleable. I mean that I change them at will when my beliefs come up against a circumstance I don't like.

I used to teach spiritual integration classes and one especially popular class was 'Forgiveness'. Those who come out of a religious experience believe in forgiveness and those who are not so religious often have a similar mindset. As human beings it makes sense to forgive others, especially as we have plenty of our own junk to be forgiven. My class was always well attended. This was a safe subject and people believed they could always leave feeling pretty good about themselves. It is easy to forgive, isn't it?

I began by having the attendees write down experiences of forgiveness in their lives, including the "who" and the "why". It would be confidential. No one would have to divulge the information to the group, but it would serve as their benchmark to start the discussion. The next step was a list of those who they needed to forgive. This exercise took longer than the first.

It was obviously more difficult. The third exercise was to write the sentence: "I can't forgive.........". Here they listed those who could never be forgiven.

The class broke into small groups of people to talk about forgiveness parts one and two. There was lots of energy and thoughtfulness. I could see people connecting with each others stories and finding their own answers in the process. Part three was saved for last when everyone got back into the large circle.

This is what they had to do in part three. I can/can't forgive (Hitler, The Terrorists of 9/11 and a few others). The room went totally silent and no one made eye contact. Finally we talked about why we might be stuck. What did this say about our collective, comfortable beliefs? There are people who are not easy to forgive and some who we are not ready to forgive. Maybe some don't "deserve" forgiveness?

There is a disconnect between what I know is right and healing, but which I am not ready to do. Those lives damaged by abuse should never be shamed or forced to forgive. It is not the message they get. There are double messages around us that if we are "good" we will be able to forgive. It exacerbates the shame for many.

If we have tucked away into the darkest recesses of our mind or attics of our soul, events and people who we need to forgive, we will arrive at the winter of our lives still weighed down. Forgiveness is a way for us to relinquish the power other people have over our lives. Without forgiveness we carry our anger, hatred, and resentments on our backs. It impacts all that we do.

Forgiveness is never about others. It does not redeem them. It does not heal them. Most of all it does not lessen their accountability. It heals us.

"We cannot help the birds of sadness flying over our heads, but we need not let them build nests in our hair"

Chinese Proverb

Forgiveness

For the most part we all get to retirement age with baggage. You can't have lived sixty years and not have brought with you all the flotsam and jetsam of living that long.

We can bury all the feelings of hurt, personal injustice and anger while we are working because work can serve as a numbing kind of drug. We get busy and forget about it. Once in a while the feelings may surface. It may be so overwhelming that they need to be handled by therapy. They must be addressed.

Forgiveness is a concept, which is not unfamiliar to all of us. The first person we need to forgive is ourselves. It keeps us from wasting time beating ourselves up for things we have done or left undone. Then we can move on and figure out how to let go of the rest.

Remember that forgiveness is not about others. It is a way to unload the beast that walks along side of us. It allows our full potential to find its creative and best self. It heals us so we can create the new me that I have been visioning.

Questions

Can I forgive myself? Grant myself permission to be myself?

Can I transform all the energy I use up in anger and pain

into something good and healing for myself?

Action

Write yourself a letter of forgiveness.

Ritual Red

I studied for my masters degree late in life. Well, relatively late, I was over fifty. One of my classmates was shocked to hear that I was "older than her mother!" I can't even remember what the impetus was, or how I got there. I just know it gave me a greater sense of accomplishment than my undergraduate program.

I went to a Catholic University and the person in charge of each candidate's masters thesis was a vision of Friar Tuck. Robust, but not as jolly as his look-alike, he was very serious about his job. When it was time to give the thesis committee the subject of my thesis: "Attending to the Spiritual in The Therapeutic Setting", he said "Never! It was not scientific. I would never find enough research material to support my thesis. Science and Psychology do not mix with spirituality. There was not enough scientific research material to qualify it as a true psychological paper". By the time he said no, I had already done enough research to write a paper longer than any Michener book. I believed in what I was writing and persisted.

I argued that we as human beings are complex, multifaceted creatures; that the mind cannot be healed without including care for the body. In addition, you cannot fix the mind without recognizing that we are spiritual beings. This holistic approach was pretty much on the fringe in the 1990's so it was an uphill battle. My advisor and the committee had many meetings with me, surveying my research and my writing. I had to defend every idea I had about treating psychological problems. I did not know until very late in the process whether they were going to accept my paper or make me begin again.

Truly, I was perplexed to hear someone who wore the frock of the church say that psychological healing would never, never include spirituality. After all, isn't that what they were living every day? I didn't mean to be religious in a therapy setting. I believed that in order to be whole we need to address people's belief systems. My friends in the program thought I was nuts and told me to just take the high road. Pick something else and get on with it. Psychology was very self-conscious about being regarded as a science. Today things are changing.

The day of my boards, I went to the room early and claimed the head of the table. I was wearing red. The committee came and sat around me. The process took longer for me than it did for most, but I passed. When they advised me, I asked if I could read the poem I had written for the occasion. They were surprised but they allowed it. I claimed my victory. I was, after all, wearing red.

Ritual Red

Hushed am I
Waiting with know-not breath
And feelings as raw and ripe
As a Christmas pomegranate.

The wait is long
And the walk is even longer to
Sit in rigid rows of expectancy
And listen for crystal sounds.

This is my ritual
For everything which has an
Ending has its own ritual of closing
And I am wearing red.

This time is mine
Mine alone to sing my song
In careful tones and solid confidence
That I am the celebrant

Thus I wore red
A cardinal about to do mass
To sing the ritual and speak the words
And lead the music to its end

It is and will be
My own song
And I am wearing red
And it is my mass

Autumn 1996

Voice

Many of us were silenced as children and continued the practice throughout our lives. Our mothers felt it necessary to keep their children quiet so as not to disturb other grownups. It also proved to others that they were good mothers and had taught their children well.

Look around you. Notice how many people at fifty or sixty are still following those teachings? It formed an idea in the "little person", who then carried it into adulthood: "In order to be loveable or valuable they must be silent." Adding to this belief is the pervasive belief "I need to be silent as I have nothing worthwhile to say." The perfect adult is mute for fear of disturbing or offending someone else. I have heard so many people say, "I hate confrontation; I will do all possible to avoid it."

Finding your voice takes courage. It takes a strong belief in self to be open to disagree, to risk expressing a point of view and to stand up against the power and energy of another person or group. You have to rock the boat and it is pretty scary.

Questions

Do you trust your own point of view?

Does the inner critic silence your voice?

Action

Find places and situations where you are an expert.

Talk. See how it feels.

Rock On

If you thought Emelda was bad with her obsession for shoes, you'd better sit down for this one. I have a "thing" for rocks. Really! Size and shape don't even matter.

I can't remember when this started exactly, but I know as I became a gardener I began a serious love affair with rocks. Rocks are the bones of every great garden and all the softscape serves only as a handmaiden to the structure. Maybe it is because I grew up in Asia where every garden celebrated the hardscape with several perfectly placed rocks. I was a tomboy, so most days I would head out into the mountains with my friends and explore the rock formations.

I don't believe for a minute this is a unique fetish. There are historical precedents for this peculiar interest, after all. Rocks have been used in ancient religions and in sacred texts for centuries. Think about it, the disciple Peter's name means 'rock'. Christianity is not, however, the only religion which uses rocks as a metaphor.

Many years ago while on a trip around The Great Lakes, I found many Inuksuk as I explored. Inuksuk can be found in ancient cultures in Alaska, Bora Bora, Russia and many other places. Inuksuk are intentionally placed and balanced piles of rocks, which tell a traveler "the way" or mark an occasion. They have spiritual meanings to the Inuit people. The Easter Islands have a ring of giant monoliths whose purpose is still somewhat fuzzy. In addition there is Stonehenge – large rocks in a circle that were used for ancient rituals. Their construction reflects people's connection to the stars and the rotation of the earth about 2,000 B.C.

I only mention this because I need some justification for my obsession. On a recent trip back to Florida from Minnesota I packed in my carry-on bag a large piece of Basalt, which I had purchased for a kings ransom at a local nursery. I didn't want it damaged in my regular luggage. It never occurred to me it could be used as a weapon. Duh. The TSA inspector didn't quite understand my theory. He threatened to dispose of it. It would have been a waste of an exquisite piece of basalt. Basalt is found in hexagonal shapes, which can grow to a very large size. Their unusual shape and color makes them an excellent accoutrement for some of Florida's beautiful butterfly ginger. I guess the look on the face of the TSA dude was pretty priceless when I think back on it. The only reason I was able to save the Basalt was I had also packed a jar of homemade jam in the same carry-on. Opps. He was satisfied with the jam and the basalt now stands tall and proud in my ginger beds.

I have recently taken to begging friends who are vacationing in Northern climes to bring me a rock or two in their cars. At this point in my life, my friends have accepted the fact I am somewhat eccentric so they laugh and humor me. Boy, you should see some of the great rocks I am collecting.

"Rocks, not just for driveways any more!"

Passions

It is not enough to dream.

My son has a quote over his desk, "There comes a time in every project when you have to fire the engineers and get on with the project."

My neighbors, however, are appalled to see me on my knees in the grass weeding at six-thirty am. It only becomes understandable when I tell them it is my form of golf. A dear friend of mine always wanted to be an artist. She created dozens of notebooks with ideas for paintings. Retired for two years now, she has not put a brush to paper. She discovered she has found a passion for other things.

There is a difference between dreaming and doing. We can dream of fishing but there comes a time to fire the engineers and get a line in the water.

Questions

What are your passions?

Who are the engineers in your mind?

Action

Do it!

Wrong Way on a One-Way Street

It was one of those wonderful *"Beaver Cleaver"* days in Hong Kong 1956. This Saturday morning was different than most. We were going to fly my new Chinese butterfly kite with a four foot wingspan.

My mother asked the cook to put together a little picnic lunch, which he packed in the wicker picnic hamper along with two red plaid thermoses full of juice. My father packed up our Morris Oxford with a picnic, my mom, two brothers, myself and the kite. We rolled down the windows and drove down Prince Edward Road toward the airport. I could hardly wait to take the beautiful golden orange and white butterfly kite out of the trunk and watch it fly. The wingspan on the kite measured nearly as wide as I was tall at 11, but then again I was short for my age.

Saturday morning in Kowloon City was the busiest day of the week. Market vendors set up their wares along the sidewalks where the Chinese housewives or their servants pick up everything they need for the coming week. Children congregated in the side streets shouting and laughing as they dodged disgruntled people trying to make their way to the stalls. On the weekends, sides of freshly butchered pig hung in stalls next to stalls of toilet paper, clothing, vegetables and other sundries in riotous bursts of color. The residents of this area, mostly Cantonese, were typically a noisy lot. Add cars honking, diesel buses, vendors yelling and planes overhead on their approach for landing and Kowloon City was a noisy bustling place.

Carefully, my father made his way through the melee and past the entrance to the airport. We had been in Hong Kong now for over five years and he was finally comfortable driving on the left side of the road. Past the airport the population thinned so we moved faster. There was little here but some industry, which supported airport services.

The narrow opening for the mountain road peeked from between two small faded white houses on my left. It was not a well-traveled road because it was narrow and rarely maintained. It was probably a cart path at an earlier time, but now it was designated a one-way road. Dad nudged the car into a lower gear and bumped through the potholes and debris littering the beginning of the road. During typhoon season, the water running down the mountain often washed away parts of the soft unkempt track. I held my breath and closed my eyes to avoid seeing how close we were to the edge. My mother was equally silent. I knew she hated heights. Her seat in the front left gave her the best view of the drop to the valley and the parts of the road which had been washed out. Dad was oblivious; he never seemed to be afraid of anything.

After climbing slowly we rounded a sharp bend and found ourselves on an open hillside. The view south across the China Sea was brilliant. The haze gone, we could see all the way to Lantau Island. Kai Tak airport lay at our feet, runway number 13 stretching into the ocean perpendicular to the shore. It seemed like a huge gray exclamation point embedded into the dark blue of the ocean.

We kids piled out of the car as soon as it stopped, delighted with the view. We stood in the wind with our arms spread like birds ready to take off. Mom sat for a while in the car while dad unloaded the picnic basket and the kite. He spread out a Chinese quilt in the grass holding down the corners with the picnic basket and a dark amber bottle of wine. I was ready to fly the kite immediately but mother, now out of the car with a silk scarf to protect her hairdo, had another plan - eat first and fly the kite later. *Why do grownups have to be so practical? I want to do the fun thing first and they can lollygag with the wine and food later!* As usual, my mother's wishes prevailed and we dutifully sat on the quilt and snarfed down the cook's chubby stuffed sandwiches. Finished, we kids wandered off along the road to explore while our parents relaxed with their wine.

Finally, it was time. My brothers and I sat cross legged by the kite, holding it down in the breeze while dad tied special knots onto the cross braces. My job was to hold it into the wind once it was secure.

"Don't forget to duck when you let go, or you might get hit by the kite as it lifts in the wind", he shouted seven or eight feet away from me. Without waiting, the wind tore the kite from my light grasp and sailed into the air with the ease of a real butterfly. Her orange and red wings fluttered in the breeze and I could hear the hum of the kite string pulling out of the bamboo spool holder. Dad braced himself, his back to the wind, while the kite climbed into the sky.

The butterfly began its long journey out beyond the edge of the hills. It was so high it looked to me like an exotic bird perched in the air waiting to capture something below. I jumped up and down yelling, "Further, further". My kite is free. All I wanted was to stand there and watch, mesmerized. Suddenly, a fierce gust came over the hill and pushed the kite to her limit. The string snapped. I gasped as she flew off, free of her strings. She was on her own.

Dad watched for a while and then turned to us. "OK, I am not in the mood for the long drive back. Given the fact that the light is going, the road is not very safe and we don't know what faces us on the road ahead, I am going to go back the way we came!". I couldn't see my mother's face, but I knew she wasn't happy.

"You are kidding? It is a one-way road!", she said protesting. No one ever argued with my dad and won. When he made up his mind, there was no changing it. In fact, arguing hardened his resolve.

It was very quiet in the car as dad turned the Morris around on the mountain edge and headed back toward town. *What will we do if we run into another car? What happens if we get caught? I am pretty sure I will not go to jail, but I am afraid none-the-less.* Dad turned the lights on and drove as close to the hill as possible. This time my mother was on the mountain side of the car and my dad on the "roll-off-into-the-great-abyss" side. Finally we saw the two small houses that marked the entrance to the airport road. We all breathed a sigh of relief. We were safe. Not a word was spoken all the way home.

Years later, as a single mother, I realized there was no milk in the fridge for breakfast. My boys were old enough to be left alone, but I had never been to the grocery store at ten o'clock at night. I didn't even know that people went out at that time of the night. Maybe the grocery store wasn't open at that ridiculous hour. I broke the 'stay-at-home-after-nine p.m. rule' and went to the store. Can you believe it? There were lots of people, even some with children, there. I bought my milk and came home.

What other rules should I learn to break that don't make sense for me? Could I finally choose to go the wrong way on a one-way street? There are people in the history books who broke the rules and became famous. They followed their instincts and hunches without allowing others to rule them. Christopher Columbus found America that way. Women who believed they should have equal rights broke the "rules" to claim it. Rosa Parks knew she should be allowed to sit anywhere on the bus.

There are rules that we can break every day without creating danger to others. I certainly don't suggest we all drive the wrong way on a one-way road. There are times, it seems to me, we should question the rules. Maybe it is time to disobey.

Breaking The Rules

Our generation grew up with rules. We were mandated by our families to follow them. It gave me high anxiety to watch my father break them at his discretion. It was a conflict for me until I was much older.

We were the generation who started the "break the rules movement". Women burned their bras and expected equal pay for equal work. What was a strange concept before, is now expected. It brought with it a "Pandora's box" of good and bad which we have lived to see in the lives of our children and grandchildren.

In the autumn of our lives we are forced to look at life in different ways. We believed retirement was the prize; our children would come to see us on Sundays for dinner and our grandchildren would call to see how we are doing. This is the "New World" for us because the rules have changed.

It is helpful to reconsider each idea which holds you back from enjoying your autumn. Some things prevent you from redefining yourself. You might find some old rules don't make sense for you anymore. There is no more time to "think about it". It is time to find your own path. Others may think you are going the wrong way on a one-way road. Just follow your instincts.
Break the Rules!

Questions

What rules have you always followed and need to change?

Is your adult in charge of the rules?

Action

As you meet them, break them as necessary

Zeitgeists

I have always been interested in words. Don't ask me, I haven't figured it out yet. I remember being in junior high and having people tell me I used big words they didn't understand. It didn't endear me to others, so obviously I didn't do it to impress them.

Do you think some people are born with a natural proclivity for words, like some are born to play basketball? It did make me popular in English class or when Trivial Pursuit became the fad. My brain was, and still is, full of the most trivial details. When I can't remember what I had for breakfast, I can usually remember the name of Boswell's dog.

When I began my masters program, I remember how many strange words there were in the reading. I was an older student and worried that I would never get the hang of all those technical terms. Of course I was wrong. The words began to make sense and I got back an enthusiasm for those little crumbs on the page. This was when I fell in love with the word "zeitgeist". Those Germans sure have a way with language. Zeitgeist, I came to understand, means "some indication of change in the environment, culture, society, nature". What a delicious word to indicate the presence of change in our world.

Of course "zeitgeists" made perfect sense to me living in the north. In Minnesota I was surrounded by "zeitgeists" after all. We had four seasons there, something we don't seem to have in Florida. The birds flocking together over the fields and ponds in the autumn; the smell of the earth warming in the spring; the graying of the skies after the leaves had washed off the trees in the late fall, all these were zeitgeists. I, who spent hours in the out-of-doors gardening, knew all these things and was thrilled to find such an interesting word to explain them. What I didn't recognize at that point was that zeitgeists are not only found "out in the world" but inside ourselves. We see it in children as they mature and physically change, but we forget somewhere along the line about those road markers in our own bodies.

It was a shock for me when I finally saw these show up in my life and I recognized them as the zeitgeists of my body aging. At 55, I think, my face was fairly wrinkle free; at least in retrospect, but one morning there they were. What happened and what did it mean? My mother told me I was not using the right face cream, so I went out and bought some. Did not change things.

I have been dying my hair red since I was 50 so I never saw the gray hairs arrive. I began to notice at a certain point the dye wasn't sticking to the new gray hairs growing around my temples. These days if you sit in a room of seniors, you will see many red headed women over 50. Now it is harder to push out of a low chair and my knees complain when I spend too long weeding in the garden. My prescriptions include cholesterol medicine, I have to watch my sugar intake as well as check my blood pressure from time to time.

At one point, I thought all zeitgeists were awesome - romantic even. Now I have developed a kind of love/hate relationship with them. I don't like them applying to my body, my life and me unless they remind me how young and vibrant I am. So was it really Eleanor Roosevelt who said, "Growing old isn't for sissies"? Well, I googled it, guess it was Bob Hope. He was right.

Markers

Make a list of your own Zeitgeists. How do you know?

Are you paying attention to the markers in your environment?

OMG – TV

Ohhh…..emmmmm……gheeeee!! Really? I think we have carried this "reality" thing on TV to a point of looking like cultural idiots. Unfortunately it makes me feel like June Cleaver on a sour balls. If the 60's was a time of doing what "felt good"; and the 70's was about excess, then the 2000's will be about being rude, contentious and self-serving in the media.

Where did it all change and when did it happen? I guess like every trend, it started quietly with the cash cow of the Simpson murder trial. Like any carnivore, we got a taste of blood and loved it. We didn't want to go back to the family fun series of the 60's because it was too "nice" and vanilla. Give us people behaving like we would never dream of behaving. It sent our adrenalin pumping and we could secretly peek into the lives of depraved, self involved, hyperbole-type people and get our darker needs met. Millions of people who never watched TV in the daytime hours spent months watching this new type of reality show unfold. We liked it and we wanted more.

Sure, it didn't happen overnight, but many day-time talk shows realized there was lots of money to be had if they presented the ugly, steamy side of life. They began to search under rocks for the ugliest and worst. Heck, America loved it when a popular host's nose was broken on live TV by some out-of-control, angry guest whose mother never taught him how to behave in public. Blood lust...maybe it touched our oldest "pack" impulses and we realized it was better than any drug we could buy on the street.

It has softened a little, thank goodness. Now we have to watch spoiled, bratty self-centered people berate others. We enjoy seeing them whine and cry because things didn't go well. Other choices include over-indulged, over-botoxed women from any big city you wish to name make "f...ing" remarks about the other women on the show. I was stunned when one woman told her friend that she had gone into the Mercedes dealer and found such a "cute" car that she bought one in every color. Waaaaaa. I am sad that we are once again making women look empty and vapid.

OK, I know I sound bitter and angry. I see children hungry, people out of work, families living on the street while we are taking heavy doses of TV-Valium so we can forget about the real reality. Hummm....maybe that is a double negative. How do I know so much, yup, I watch some of that stuff just so that I can bellyache about how depraved television has become.

Excuse me but it is time for my favorite shrink. He and another host collaborated on a family who…, well, let me get back to you on that plot. I have a TV show to watch.

BBFN.

Sedatives

TV is a perfect example of how we deceive ourselves into believing we have accomplished something. In truth we are numbing ourselves out with nonsense. Right now there is nothing on television that is socially redeeming. Redeeming in the sense that it is not worth your precious time. I will agree there are a few substantive things from time to time. Things which make us better people and more sensitive to the world around us. We would be better served by talking to a friend or volunteering in our community. We have the choice to watch someone else improve the world and pay it forward, or we can decide to do it ourselves.

Depression, boredom and many kinds of stress cause us to emotionally check out. It is difficult to define them or even recognize them. It happens as a subtle shift in our behaviors and feelings. Large changes will have a natural period of grief and loss; the most important thing is to recognize it happening and know when it has lasted too long. The lesson in all of this – be the actor not the audience.

Questions

What is your sedative of choice?

How do you identify it?

What can and will you do about it?

Action

Make a commitment to participate in something.

Shadowlands

So many of us love the work of C.S. Lewis. What child isn't enthralled by *The Lion, The Witch and The Wardrobe*? All of those magical times by brave, heroic children whose very lives changed as they stepped through that wardrobe. What is ironic about Lewis is that he wrote mostly of his own faith journey. He laid out his beliefs in stories and metaphors, which addressed change and transformation mostly for scholars and spiritual academics. However, many of us have been deeply moved by his stories whether we understood the spiritual tone of them or not. Then again, maybe we have to be in touch with the child in ourselves to hear the depth of his words.

There is a fountain in Oslo's Frogner Park, which celebrates the work of Gustav Vigeland. One of the most touching sculptures, to me, is the 'Tree of Life' fountain. It features many human figures around the edge of the fountain at various stages of life. My favorite is a sapling with a female child in its branches. This child is ready and ripe to become a woman and is throwing herself from the branches into "life". The girl is neither an innocent child nor a fully realized woman. She hangs suspended between both worlds, not in one place or the other.

She exists in both worlds but is not yet transformed. She is fearless.

Anthony Hopkins, who plays Lewis in the movie "Shadowlands", talks about the part of the day in which all things are in between time. In a doorway between rooms, not yet on either side. That time of the day when the world is devoid of color but not yet dark.

Transformation and change is something we all experience in the long list of our days. In fact, isn't the act of being born the first and most traumatic of changes in our experience? Vigeland celebrated the changes in each stage of life, knowing that it was a universal human experience. Often we are not even aware of change, and we slide effortlessly into the next stage without notice. There are times when change makes us cry out. We resist with all of our energy, against a flooded river of uncertainty. Newness requires us to be different; to throw ourselves out of that tree into the unknown and trust that it will be fine. It is in that moment we pause in the shadowlands of our mind and heart, knowing we have no choice.

Yet resisting ...we pause.

Being In-Between

At dinner the other night someone asked my friend how old she was. We all know it was not a politically correct thing to do, but then again, some of us just dive into questions without thinking. She was very gracious and answered, "I am seventy-nine...and a half." We all laughed.

Not since we were four...and a half or eight...and a half have we counted those times. You never hear someone say "I am thirty and a half"! At some point we are cognizant of the fact that to reach a certain mile marker is an accomplishment. We are between two important times in our lives and we unabashedly speak our age. Even halves.

Question

What are you between?

How do you know that you are transitioning?

Action

Name it. _____.

Southern Rules

I read the other day that the 'Millennium Man" has "C.I.I." - confused identity issues! One evening of TV and you see the trend that portrays men as stupid or violent. If they cry or do laundry for the family they are less male or stupid. Well, move over you guys. I am struggling myself and I don't know where to go for direction.

I am one of those self-sufficient Northern women. I can run a variable speed reversing drill; change the ball cock on the toilet gismo and beat you at golf if you are not careful. I have to admit, though, my mother warned me not to look too smart around boys. I read *The Fear of Flying* several times and thought that Erica Jong was Strega Nona on steroids.

The problem came when I moved to the "South". I had no idea that it is a cultural state of its own. There are things here that I have never read about in my history books and their mores are very strange.

The Civil War for example, can you believe it was not really a Civil War? By Southern standards, what we rather practical northerners call that great war to abolish slavery, was not a war of conscience at all? I mean, according to my southern women friends, it was the "War of Northern Aggression". It was a power play by Northerners to stifle free trade in the south. They still hold it against us that we waged war at all and by most accounts, they did not really lose. They chose to save lives and took the moral high road.

I moved into my "southern" home before my husband finished working so I was alone in my well-heeled neighborhood. Let me tell you, I was suspect right away. After all, I was a single woman and surely needed to mind my peas and queues around the men folk. Once, when I was mowing my lawn, I saw a group of neighbors standing in the road talking. Being a friendly soul, I waved genially and moseyed over to the group to see what was going on. Not a woman in sight, only guys. Within moments, I saw female faces in the windows of nearby homes and soon some "pressing" task took them inside and out of my clutches

I did make friends with one of the ladies down the block. I could have "hated" her if she hadn't been such a wonderful person. She told me that she considered herself a typical southern woman. She never gardened without a large brimmed hat and never, never wore slacks out in public or anywhere for that matter. Her home was like a combination antique store and high end bits and bobs shop. Every wall, I mean every wall was covered with beauty! Limoges plates, hand painted cups, old paintings of Victorian women, lace geegaws and other stuff too fluffy to mention. It was always CLEAN….and you never felt uncomfortable. If she served you coffee it was in exquisite demitasse cups and little spoons with pearl handles to stir your "shuga". If you preferred sweet tea, the crystal goblets were stemmed and always came with a slice of fresh lemon. ARRRRRG.

I'm from the prairies, for goodness sake, we take the enamel coffee pot off the fire and pour the coffee into sturdy old pottery mugs with large handles. Any woman worth her salt wears jeans or even possibly overalls. Make up? Well, never once did I ever catch my friend, no matter the hour, without her makeup and hair combed. She cooked her husband a hot breakfast every morning. Over the years she shared many little southern recipes with me, like her famous "tomato pai". One secret that has been the most useful for me is the "bless-their-hearts" rule.

The "bless-their-hearts" rule is this. You may say anything about anyone as long as you follow the remark up, in a hushed voice, with "bless-their-hearts!". It is the same rule we have in the north that says if you are going to eat a huge piece of chocolate cake, wash it down with a diet drink because the calories become null. It seems that it is also not acceptable for a southern woman to use cuss words. It is all right, however, to substitute "I Suwannee" meaning I swear, when a cuss is appropriate.

Well, I don't know if I can keep up with the Southern way. I haven't worn a dress since my father's funeral. My coffee cups are service cups and the rule is that they must be able to hold half the pot. The other half goes to my husband. I just want to know how to treat for chinch bugs in my St Augustine grass and I don't want your husband. I don't own any silver that needs polishing or anything that has pearl handles.

I Suwannee, my Jacksonville friend is a wench, "bless-her-heart".

Diversity

Diversity in this instance has a much broader meaning than the "diversity" training we got at work. When you live in a retirement community you live with many kinds of diversity. Some people are militant about their lawns being manicured by a fingernail clipper, and some are much more laissez-faire about it. Some people eat out every single day and some never go out. While making new friends we bring an a la carte menu of all our foibles. Our family and those who know us may roll their eyes, but they live with us and love us anyway. Now these quirks are exacerbated.

It seems that as we get older our world becomes smaller. Maybe it is our vision and we need "social" glasses. More seniors complain about their neighbors cat or landscape than ever happened in the working world. We didn't have the time. You will discover that one friend talks incessantly which you never noticed before. Your best friend is a dreaded double dipper at the buffet. Yuk.

Those from one area of the country, who avoid conflict at all cost, are thrown into a mix of people who believe conflict is just another word for friendship. Change mandates that you learn this new kind of "diversity sensitivity".

Questions

Who drives you nuts? Why?

Can you wear beige and keep your mouth zipped?

Action

Smile and say "How nice"

Bridges

I remember reading *The Bridges of Madison County* on vacation in the Dominican Republic. I sat on a lounge chair only yards from the turquoise blue water. My feet were dusted with sand and I was bawling. A woman nearby came over to ask if I was all right. She came to comfort me because my sadness touched her. I was both embarrassed and moved by her compassion. The story was fiction after all and I happened to have a Bahama Mama on the wicker table next to me. How sad could I be? I was in a beautiful place with great friends. Why would anyone be sobbing under those circumstances? I thanked the woman for her kindness and offered her the book, as I was finished. After hearing the explanation for my tears, she didn't want to be sad on her vacation. She left it on my table.

The book triggered many things. I was moved by the deep emotional and spiritual connections Francesca experienced in those four days. I understood the moral decisions she had to make about her life. Each of us longs to be transformed by love, even if is only for a fleeting moment. In those moments we are all called to make a choice. We can choose to change and crossover the boundaries we have drawn around our lives or we can stand where we are planted and see the bridge as an option not taken. The book bridges our existential loneliness with reality. It reminds us of what we value and who we are at the core of ourselves.

Bridges, after all, speak to us. They inspire and serve us. Who isn't awed by the amazing red Golden Gate Bridge peaking out of a blanket of fog into the clear blue sky for an instance? A bridge is a tangible metaphor for a joining or a transition. It serves as a reminder that two cities, countries or even two ideologies can be transformed or joined by a metaphoric structure.

I have chosen the autumn bridge for the cover of my book because I too am in a time of transition and transformation. The change from busy work life to retirement is exciting and frightening. I thought it would be easy, but there was more to it than I ever imagined. Crossing over means taking time to check out what I want to do. What makes me happy? What am I going to do with the next thirty years of my life? Can I give birth to myself in new and exciting ways? A female theologian I read years ago said, "When a woman's womb becomes dark and dusty, she gives birth to herself." I don't remember who the speaker was, but I do remember every day I am pregnant with potential.

We are shape-shifters on this journey. How we cope with change and what we do with it will determine if our autumn years are zesty and meaningful. What are you going to do with this golden time? The bridge is there, see where it leads.

"The world will provide you with stones every day;

what you build out of them is your choice – a bridge or a wall".

Unknown

Suggested Reading List - Bibliography

Aging:

Cohen M.D, Gene. *2001. The Creative Age-Awakening Human Potential in The Second Half of Life.*

Hill, Robert D. 2008. *Seven Strategies for Positive Aging.*

Lindbergh, Reeve. 2002. *No More Words: A Journal of My Mother, Anne Morrow Lindbergh.*

Pipher, Mary. 2000. *Another Country: Navigating the Emotional Terrain of Our Elders.*

Saussy, Carroll. 1998. *The Art of Growing Old.*

Schacter-Shalomi, Zalman and Miller, Ronald S. 1997. *From Ageing to Sage-ing: A Profound New Vision of Growing Older.*

Vaillant, George E. 2003. *Aging Well: Surprising Guideposts to a Happier Life.*

Weil M. D., Andrew 2007. *Healthy Aging: A Lifelong Guide to Your Well-Being.*

Spirituality:

Durek, Judith. 2004. *Circle of Stones: Woman's Journey to Herself.*

Fischer, Kathleen. 1998. *Winter Grace: Spirituality and Aging.*

Kidd, Sue Monk. 2006 *When the Heart Waits: Spiritual Direction for Life's Sacred Questions.*

Lindbergh, Anne Morrow. 1991. *Gift From the Sea.*

Rohr, Richard. 2011 *Falling Upward: A Spirituality for The Two Halves of Life.*

Williamson, Marianne. 1996. *A Return To Love: Reflections on the Principles of A Course in Miracles.*

Retirement

Rutgers University Press. 2003. *Women Confronting Retirement: A Nontraditional Guide.*

Dodds, Bill. 2000. *What You Don't Know About Retirement: A Funny Retirement Quiz.*

Kuchler, Bonnie Louise. 2009. *Retirement is a Full-Time Job: And You're the Boss.*

Lloyd, Mary. 2009. *Supercharged Retirement: Ditch the Rocking Chair, Trash the Remote, and Do What You Love.*

Stone, Marika and Stone, Howard. 2004. *Too Young to Retire: 101 Ways to Start the Rest of Your Life.*

Zelinski, Ernie J. 2009. *How to Retire Happy, Wild and Free: Retirement Wisdom That You Won't Get from Your Financial Advisor.*

Inspiration:

Bratter, Bernice and Dennis, Helen. 2008. *Project Renewal.*

Bridges, William. 1980. *Transitions: Making Sense of Life's Changes.*

Carlson, Richard. 1997. *Don't Sweat The Small Stuff...and it's all small stuff.*

Frankl, Viktor E. 1984. *Man's Search for Meaning.*

Johnson, Spencer and Blanchard, Kenneth. 1998. *Who Moved My Cheese?: An Amazing Way to Deal with Change in Your Work and Your Life.*

Norris, Kathleen. 1993. *Dakota: A Spiritual Geography.*

Katherine Edwins Schumm

Katherine has been a storyteller all her life. As a counselor she worked with women and children in transition and presented workshops on grief and loss.

In 2000 at the "Women at Midlife Conference" at St. Catherine's University in St. Paul she was a featured speaker for Creating Circles of Intention at Midlife : Ways to find meaningful friendships for supporting life's changes. Her article Ode to Joy about her paternal grandparents mission in China was published worldwide in the magazine "Spotlight on China" in 2002. Retired in 2003, she moved to Florida with her husband and three rescued dogs.

Made in the USA
San Bernardino, CA
30 April 2017